New You

A Proven System to Turn Your Dreams into Reality

Abner Amador

Contents

Dedication

To my father,

From whom I learned
to strive for a dream
even when it seemed beyond reach

To never give up and stay the course
believing it could be done

Thank you for always
trusting me with so much more
that I could ever had trusted myself

Preface

Welcome to a journey of turning dreams into tangible realities. In these pages, you'll find more than a guide; you'll discover a system born from personal experiences and a relentless pursuit of aspirations. This book is not a manual for success but rather a companion in the pursuit of dreams.

As the author, I invite you to delve into a world where dreams are not distant ideals but the driving force behind intentional actions. The system presented here is not a one-size-fits-all solution, but rather a flexible framework waiting to be adapted to your unique journey.

In sharing my stories and the insights gained from navigating the path from dreams to reality, I hope to ignite a spark within you. Whether you're standing at the threshold of a new project, a career change, or a personal transformation, these pages hold the tools to guide you.

Dreams are the seeds of change, and this book could be the fertile soil that nurtures their growth in your life. It's an exploration of dreams as tangible entities, waiting for the right combination of decisions and action from each of us to blossom into the extraordinary.

My hope is that these words resonate with you, spark your creativity, and propel you forward on your journey of dream realization. Here's to embracing the challenges, savoring the victories, and, most importantly, making your dreams come true.

-Abner Amador

Foreword

Lake Washington, Seattle, WA 2015

Nine years ago, back in 2015, I was hired by an international consulting firm to join a project in Seattle, WA. I had been living in Monterrey, Mexico for 30 years and had never worked in the United States. Our company ended up selecting and sending about 15 people from Mexico to work on this project in Seattle for one year and I felt lucky to be part of this team and excited about the opportunity. I had never really planned to work in the USA, specially at the age of 48, but when the opportunity came up I was more than ready to make the most of it.

When I arrived in Seattle, it was the month of June and the weather was perfect to explore the amazing emerald city. I remember focusing completely on my new work assignment and learning the new skills and tools needed to be successful at my new job from Monday to Friday, but knowing that I was going to be in Seattle for only one year, I decided to spend my weekends getting to know Seattle, its neighborhoods and natural wonders.

On my third weekend, I remember walking by one of the water canals on the north side of the city and seeing several people kayaking and doing stand up paddle boarding. Back in Mexico I had never seen anyone doing either of these activities, but being raised in Tampico, a city by the Gulf of Mexico, I had always enjoyed spending time at the beach, swimming in the ocean or at the lake next to the sport facilities where my siblings and I would often attend for swimming lessons. In other words, any water activity would immediately attract me.

After figuring out where to rent a kayak, I tried that activity for the first time. It was a beautiful sunday afternoon. I made sure to had someone at the rental place take my photo as a memoir to this activity that felt so casual to anyone in Seattle but felt huge for me. The first 20 minutes when well as I found my way around the water and decided in which direction to go, until things didn't go as expected when I ended up on a section of the lake where the boats have to go under a bridge creating more waves that I could handle making the water very choppy.

My kayak ended up flipping and I had to spend the next twenty minutes figuring out how to get back in it while trying to get the water out of it. The task became frustrating and decided to begin waving for help. Thankfully two guys going bye on jet skies pulled up and one of them was kind enough to help me out and show me how to use a pump that I had not even seen inside the kayak to get the water out. I decide to go to the nearest shore and regain a bit of my strength back from the struggle on trying to get back on the kayak. Finally, I made it back to the rental place, returned the equipment and left with bittersweet taste from the experience. What was supposed to be a fun activity, now had me wondering if I should even consider trying it again.

It was not until about two months later on a different part of town, that I decided to rent a stand up paddle board for the first time. I supposed enough time had gone bye that allowed me to regain the courage to try for another water activity that I had never done before.

After about 3 minutes on the board, I decided to go from kneeling to standing and in less than a minute I lost my balance and fell in the water. I immediately remembered my first experience on the kayak but something happened right after that. Instead of feeling frustrated and scared as I did with a flipped kayak full of water, falling from the stand up paddle board actually felt fun! I remember thinking - the worst that could happen has already happened (I got wet) and now I can just enjoy learning how to to keep my balance on the board.

That was the beginning of what became not just my favorite hobby in Seattle but the one activity that allowed me to explore amazing spots in the Seattle area full of lakes, and allowed me also to make new friends plus teach other how to paddle board for the first time (something I need several times with coworkers and their families).

Towards the end of my first year in Seattle, I found out that there was the possibility to extend my contract on that same project for another year along with most of my co-workers from Mexico. To complete the process, each of us had to come back to Mexico, visit the US Consulate, renew our work visa for another year and go back to Seattle. This same process happened three times in the following years, so I ended up working four years instead of just one for the company that brought me to Seattle.

In 2019, a different company hired me and helped me go through the lengthy process of getting my residence card (better known as "green card"), which thankfully after two and a half year was completed and has allowed me to now live indefinitely in the United States.

How did any of these things happened?

As you reflect on your personal life, you might look back at key events or moments while asking yourself the same question I have asked myself plenty of times over the last nine years…how did any of these amazing things ever happened?

Considering that there are so many factors that have a direct impact on our lives but seem to be completely up to other and totally beyond our individual control, another way to look at the same question is if any of us as individuals in the vast universe of possibilities are able to have any influence or capacity to direct or redirect the destiny of our lives!

Although I might not have all the answers, there are two things I know for sure.

First of all, I am certain that as human beings, we have the capacity to dream, and project in our minds a version of our lives that becomes intentional. This process alone, allows us to explore things that otherwise we would not even take time to consider.

Secondly, the more I reflect on the process to make dreams come true, the easier and more obvious things seem to be, so looking out "reliability" and "consistency" in our actions will be fundamental to unlocking the benefits from the system described in this book.

My hope, as you immerse yourself in the depths of the ideas and experiences that I share in each chapters in this book, is for you to be inspired and be able to reflect on your own life and the way you currently approach your dreams and the decisions that have brought to where you are today.

Good or bad, any destination in life is just another opportunity to stop, think and decide where to go next…

And just like I have done in the past few months, by reflecting on the last nine years of my life, I encourage you to do the same for your life allowing this book to be a guide and a coaching aid to enhance the way you approach life to design and empower the 'New You'.

-Abner Amador

Introduction

Creating a Consistent and Reliable "System" for Making Dreams Come True

Let's debunk the mystery around the term "system" since it is a concept more familiar than you might think. When you encounter the word "system," envision something in your life that's rock-solid and dependable – much like your car, watch, or phone.

Consider a car, a marvel of interconnected components – an engine, wheels, seats – working seamlessly to transport you, not just once, but repeatedly to the grocery store, work, fun places and beyond. It's a finely tuned "vehicle", or transportation system, designed for a specific purpose, with essential parts collaborating for a common goal.

While parts of the system have been added over time to make it more comfortable or satisfy additional needs like adding a radio so you can listen to music or the news, these are not essential to the basic original purpose. Identifying "key" or "essential" components for the system we are trying to create will be the focus of the first part of this book, spanning Chapters 1-5.

Another great example of a system is the kitchen in your home. Kitchens have existed for thousands of years, with key components remaining constant despite evolving appearances due to technological changes: storage for food, cold storage for perishables, fire or heating devices, plates, cups and tools for washing and cleaning.

Looking at a kitchen from a fresh perspective

By thinking about your kitchen as a system, the important lesson to be remembered is that the correct interaction of the elements in your kitchen can consistently deliver your expectations. In other words, a kitchen can be described as a system to feed people, or better yet, a system to make "Culinary Dreams" come true!

Kitchen - a system to make "Culinary Dreams" come true

Photo by Naomi Hébert on Unsplash

7 Key Principles to keep in mind while you read this book.

1. Unlimited Human Potential:

At the heart of our journey lies the recognition of the boundless potential that resides within each one of us. The canvas of human potential knows no boundaries, and as we explore the depths of our dreams, we uncover the vast landscapes of what we can achieve. Your potential is not confined by circumstances or limitations – it's an ever-expanding horizon waiting to be explored.

2. Ageless Dreams and Timeless Goals:

In the realm of dreams, age is but a number. Whether you're on the brink of adulthood or seasoned by the years, the power to dream and set meaningful goals remains undiminished. C.S. Lewis's timeless wisdom reminds us that every age is an opportunity for new dreams, and as we progress through life, our goals evolve, adapt, and shape the "New You."

3. Resilience in the Face of Challenges:

Life, with all its mysteries and challenges,serves as the workshop in which resilience is crafted. Each obstacle presents an opportunity to showcase the indomitable spirit residing within. As we navigate the twists and turns, we discover that challenges can be used as stepping stones toward personal growth. You are not only capable of overcoming difficulties but emerging stronger, wiser, and more resilient.

4. Unveiling Life's Mysteries:

Life is a grand mystery waiting to be unveiled. Each day presents an opportunity to uncover hidden truths, explore new possibilities, and deepen our understanding of ourselves and the world. Embrace the mystery with curiosity and an open heart, for it is in the journey of discovery that life reveals its most profound secrets.

5. Life as an Adventure:

Picture life as an exhilarating adventure, with every step forward leading to uncharted territories. The destinations may be significant, but the essence of the journey lies in the experiences gained, lessons learned, and the transformation that occurs along the way. Embrace the adventure, relish the unknown, and savor every moment of the expedition toward the "New You."

6. Embracing Change:

Change is a constant companion on the journey of life. Instead of fearing or resisting it, let's welcome change with open arms. It is through change that we evolve, grow, and redefine ourselves. Discover that change is not a threat but a powerful force propelling us toward new horizons.

7. "New You" Every Day:

The concept of the "New You" is not a distant destination; it unfolds every day. Recognize that each dawn brings the opportunity to become a better version of yourself. Life is a series of choices, and with each choice, you shape the person you are becoming. Embrace the responsibility and power that comes with daily transformation – for the "New You" is a masterpiece in progress, sculpted by your choices and actions.

Chapter One

Dreams – Boundless Possibilities

"You are never too old to set another goal or to dream a new dream."
- C.S. Lewis

In the expansive landscape of the mind, dreams are not mere whims but potent seeds of boundless potential, eagerly awaiting the fertile ground of your imagination. This chapter invites you to navigate the limitless terrain of your aspirations, challenging any beliefs that may shackle the full expression of your dreams.

Breaking Free from Limiting Beliefs

To turn dreams into reality, it is crucial to confront and dismantle the barriers within our own minds. Limiting beliefs, often shaped by past experiences or societal expectations, can create a confined space for our dreams to unfold.

As C.S. Lewis encourages, the ageless nature of dreaming implies that limitations are often self-imposed. Recognizing and challenging these constraints will be part of our reflective journey together.

With some practical exercises which you will find at the end of each chapter, you will take steps that eventually will allow you to spot and discern from emotions like fear, pain or shame which might be holding you back to expand your mind into boundless possibilities.

C.S. Lewis's Perspective on Endless Possibilities

From the enchanting world of Narnia to the philosophical depths of his essays, Lewis's writings inspire us to embrace the expansive realm of our dreams. A literary luminary and philosopher, C.S. Lewis understood the transformative power of imagination and his characters demonstrate the perspective on the limitless potential of the human mind.

How can we empower ourselves with the leverage that imagination, curiosity and creativity has provided endless writers, directors, entrepreneurs, inventors and dream-achievers in general throughout history?

We will discover our first insight from two of C.S. Lewis books and characters:

In his book, "The Lion, the Witch and the Wardrobe," the character of Lucy experiences the timeless nature of dreams when she discovers the magical world of Narnia hidden within the wardrobe. Despite being a child, Lucy's dreams lead her to a place where time seems to stand still, and she finds herself playing a crucial role in the destiny of Narnia.

Our second example can be found in "The Voyage of the Dawn Treader," where the character of Eustace Clarence Scrubb undergoes a transformative journey of self-discovery. Despite initially being skeptical and self-centered, Eustace learns valuable lessons about courage, friendship, and redemption through his adventures in Narnia.

Even if you are not familiar with the details of the characters and adventures described in great detail in each of the Narnia book collection, what is important to realize is that in order for the author to convey and communicate abstract ideas and complex thoughts like attributes and emotions to the reader, these need to be "packaged" in a way that any of us can relate to and understand - a character in his story.

By taking the shape of an imaginary human being who can talk, walk, feel and breath just like any of us, these abstract ideas and thoughts can be transmitted from the author's mind to the pages on a book and then transported to the mind of endless readers.

Creating fictional and relatable characters is a technique used by famous writers and storytellers since the dawn of time, highlighting how personal dreams can be manifested regardless of age or circumstance and ultimately leading to profound reflection that can fuel transformation, first in the imaginary world and eventually in the physical world.

The notion that dreams are not confined by time, age, or circumstance, should encourage us to dream boldly, set audacious goals, and embark on a journey of self-discovery.

As you will see next, in the pursuit of turning dreams into reality, the word 'DREAMS' will serve as first essential component of our carefully designed system. Dreaming within and beyond your current boundaries will set the stage for the transformation that lies ahead.

TAKE ACTION: STEP 1

From the many ways of practicing the art of dreaming to unlock creativity, curiosity and imagination we will start by using a practical exercise to get started. We won't be creating any fictional characters (yet), but will start with a "version of you" that is willing to dream.

The "Big Question" that helps people start Dreaming by removing self imposed restrictions:

Step 1: Take a piece of paper answer the following question:

If money and time were not an issue, what will you dream of doing in the following twelve months?

Step 2: Your list of DREAMS will most likely be fueled by either NEEDS or WANTS so start each sentence by using one of the following formats:

Want(s): I would_____

Need(s): I should_____

Don't worry about making a perfect list. You can always come back and make adjustments. Just make sure to have between 1-3 sentences that you can use as you go through each of the steps of our system.

Here is one example that we will use as an illustration for each upcoming chapter:

If money and time were not an issue, I would travel to Europe in the next 12 months.

Are you excited? Is Dreaming something that you are used to doing? Do you ever write down your dreams?

When writing down your dreams, don't let discouraging thoughts get in your way of dreaming like trying to decide if your dreams are "too big" or "too small", "realistic or unrealistic". Dreaming is a gift that all humans have been given and the more you enjoy this gift and practice it, an essential part of the "New You" will come to life.

Chapter Two

Vision – Intangible Reality

"The only thing worse than being blind is having sight but no vision."

- Helen Keller

In the boundless cosmos of life, dreams act as guiding stars, lighting our way through the unexplored realms of our potential. However, to turn these dreams into reality, we must embark on a purposeful journey – a journey paved with well-defined goals, right?

Yes, but not yet....

Let's forget about goals for now. We will come back to that topic later in this book, because "order" and "sequence" can either hinder growth or drive it. As any farmer about the terrible consequences of expecting seeds to grow in unprepared soil. Seeds are so precious but yet so fragile and so might be the case for your dreams.

The next logical step in the system we are creating to turn dreams into reality, is to take advantage of your capacity for dreaming and turn those dreams into a vision.

How is a Vision different than a Dream?

Many people, speakers, authors and books might use these two terms indifferently, almost like synonyms because they are in fact interconnected as part of our cognitive thinking process, but the reality is that Dreams can be very vague and abstract while a Vision essentially forces us to cross a layer of abstraction which we will refer to as a "decision layer" as we move on.

Crafting the Vision for the "New You" using vision sentences.

Let's use the example from chapter 1:

If money and time were not an issue, I would travel to Europe in the next 12 months.

From Intangible Abstract Ideas to Concrete Tangible Reality

Abstract thoughts travel through our minds everyday. Our senses feed us with facts, situations and experiences that allow us to have more abstract thoughts. We hear a loud noise, and begin to wonder what happened in our proximity. Did something break, did something bad happen?

As we drive down the street, we see things or people allowing our minds to collect more and more images feeding our always hungry sense-driven brains. There are other times when we are so absorbed in our inner thoughts and cognitive processes, that the images or things around us take the back stage and are not even acknowledged. Someone will ask us something and we will not respond until asked again if he "heard" what we were ask or told.

Slowing down to capture your Dreams.

Imagine your life as a blank canvas, awaiting the strokes of your aspirations and the hues of your ambitions. Before you can even decide on drawing the first line, endless ideas and thoughts cross your mind. You have to select something, you have to start making decisions as you stare at the endless possibilities.

Most life decisions are triggered by a person's urgent NEEDS and urgent WANTS, while important and not urgent NEEDS and WANTS tend to be buried in the pile of ideas waiting to make it to the top of a person's priority list.

This is why on step one, we used the two words -Needs and Wants, to help us make our first decision. By interrupting, slowing down and redirecting the traffic an the endless flow of abstract thoughts of ideas allows us to focus on one, two or three dreams.

At this point we don't need to worry about how urgent or important these dreams are.

But the step (and the time) to write them down can make a world of difference.

Slowing down the rapid spinning wheel of our cognitive process might not seem as much, but by choosing one or two dreams to further think about, you have done something incredibly important. Instead of just keep dreaming more and more, letting our imagination go wild, you have "selected" a dream or two in order to bring it down from the top most layer of abstraction. Making the decision to focus on one dream at a time can be transformative and eye-opening as you will see in the rest of this chapter.

From an Abstract Dream to a Vision

The word Vision suggests the use of one of our most powerful senses -our sight, our eyes.

And by writing down a sentence that starts with the format "I see _____", there are two possibilities:

I can be describing something real and tangible within my scope of vision, or I can be describing something I am able to visualize within the scope of my imagination.

Seeing the Future

A widely used question for a job interview is to ask a candidate "where do you see yourself in 1, 5, 10 years". Experienced recruiters and managers looking for talent know that people can't real see the future, yet they insist on asking candidates this question, not because they are looking for fortune tellers, prophets or some type of mystical leader.

The power of this question lies in being able to identify how limited or ambitious a candidate's imagination is willing to take take him/her ahead in time, virtually time traveling to contemplate and considering different possibilities, scenarios and realities by allowing a person to willingly speak and communicate abstract thoughts and ideas about the future, regardless of whether these things will ever happen.

Attitude towards describing the future can be a powerful insight to hire and bring someone to be part of a team or company. Is a person bold, positive and ambitious or pessimistic and negative?

Here is a good question to ask yourself and explore later in chapter 8. Would you hire yourself as the CEO of your life? Keep this mind as we move forward but let the chapters in between provide additional wisdom before you have to answer that question.

From an "If" statement to an "I see myself" statement

Instead of using the commonly used format of the question "where do you see yourself in X amount of time", we will use a variant of this question for our system by applying the following format to one specific dream at a time: "I can see myself…"

Take our previous chapter dream statement:

If money and time were not an issue, I would travel to Europe in the next 12 months.

then turned it into the following statement:

I can see myself traveling to Europe in the next 12 months.

Read the two phrases several times and allow your mind to capture the beauty and power of this simple change that allows us to bring an abstract idea like a dream closer to a tangible reality.

Being able to "see" something in our mind" can be seen similar to "a promise to ourselves", a projection of a possible reality which can happen by just adding this small touch of reality by calling out one of our senses, bringing our dream one step closer to reality.

In other words, if you never "see yourself" playing the lead character on the endless list of dreams that cross your mind everyday, most likely, that dream, no matter how cool or amazing, will be treated in your mind just like any other cool or amazing movie that you watch on a weekend destined to fall back into archive of unfulfilled dreams.

Aligning Dreams with Core Values

The next step that you need to take for any of your dreams to come true is make sure that it aligns with your beliefs and values.

When writing down a list of 10 things that we would like to do or think we should do, most likely there will be a few that we would immediately question, not because we are not able to continue to the process of bringing them further down into reality but because either,

A: It seems to competes or conflict with other dreams on the list. B: It does not align with who we are or want to be.

But this is totally normal since we will always be able to dream beyond what we will be capable of achieving in a lifetime. One of the big problems that people face with unrealized dreams is the frustration of not consciously taking the time to check A or B, wasting energy on the pursuit of a dream that will never happen because deeply rooted within, they don't believe in that particular dream.

Adding a WHY

Our personal belief system can be very complex. Mostly serving as a moral compass directing our decisions, every now then confusion and lack of clarity pushes us to the edge of our belief system boundaries. Am I capable of this or that? I am even supposed to consider doing something like that?

This existential dilemma of human life has prevailed as part of culture and tradition since the dawn of times. Aligning to rules and staying within social norms or boundaries vs discovering and testing those limits, where a type of approval is all we seek to continue our pursuit.

Answering WHY we can see ourselves doing something in the future, whether expected or unexpected, is crucial to allows us to continue the pursuit of a dream. Not answering or discover the WHY can endanger and undermine our willingness to push ourselves to the final stretch of our dream if we are not fully convinced that this is something we want or should do.

So, it is now time for you to take the next step and "see yourself" doing something in the future, without unveiling the reasons for the pursuit of a specific dream making plans and setting goals would just be a waste of your time and energy.

TAKE ACTION: STEP 2

The practical way to discover your why and see how this or any future dream aligns to your belief system is by adding the word "because" and coming up with ideas in the form of phrases that you can write down.

I can see myself traveling to Europe
in the next 12 months
BECAUSE _____

To turn your dream into a vision, use this practical approach:

Go from "If money or time were not an issue..." to "I see myself..." format.

Explore one or more reasons behind your dream to uncover your motivations for making it happen.

Here is an example of multiple motivations:

I can see myself traveling to Europe in the next 12 months BECAUSE…

-I've always wanted to travel there
-many of my friends have been there and I don't want to feel left out
-I've heard so many great stories about it and want to experience it myself
-I want to visit different different parts of the world every year and Europe is next
-I've met people from Europe and I want to visit the places they have recommended
-I hate where I live and maybe I should move to Europe!

Exploring your dreams while you try to turn them into a vision can be very revealing and satisfying. Don't worry if one or more of your motivations might seem negative, like the last one on the list above. As humans, our motivations can also include avoiding PAIN, SHAME or FEAR.

Going beyond our comfort zone to a discovery zone is part of the process to reinvent the 'New You', so take some time to dig into your initial list of dreams and take them one step closer to reality by turning them into a vision.

Remember, the journey of transforming your dreams into a vision is a powerful step towards unveiling the extraordinary potential within you and becoming the person you aspire to be.

Adding the WHY for your Vision will make you aware of your motives. We all have NEEDED or WANTED something in life that we didn't end up pursuing but waste precious time and energy planning for it and setting goals. Maybe it was because we never took the time to explore our MOTIVATION(S) behind our dream making sure there was alignment with our personal internal belief system.

Believing in yourself and knowing what you believe in is essential to unlocking the dreams that will turn into the vision of your 'New You'.

Chapter Three

Plans - Options & Alternatives

"Success is not final, failure is not fatal: It is
the courage to continue that counts."
- Winston Churchill

In our quest to pursue our dreams, we inevitably encounter obstacles that test our resolve and challenge our commitment as life unfolds like a grand tapestry, woven with threads of both ups and downs, triumphs and tribulations.

Facing Challenges with Resilience

Resilience is the cornerstone of overcoming obstacles, and like the mythical cat with its nine lives, we have the capacity within us to bounce back from setbacks and transform hardships into stepping stones toward our dreams.

The Myth of Nine Lives: Insights from Feline Tenacity

The concept of a cat having nine lives serves as a captivating metaphor for tenacity and survival. Firstly, cats are renowned for their remarkable agility and survival skills. They often seem to emerge unscathed from precarious situations, such as high falls or dangerous encounters. This resilience and seemingly fearless nature have contributed to the belief that cats possess multiple lives.

As you navigate through this chapter, visualize the obstacles in your path not as impossible hurdles, but as chances to draw upon your inner strength. Much like the legendary cat with its multiple lives, let it serve as a reminder of the unwavering resilience that resides within you. "New You" emphasizes that setbacks aren't the conclusion of your journey, but rather vital chapters in the story of transforming dreams into reality. Embrace these challenges, and allow yourself to reset your life as many times as needed in order to keep moving on.

PLANS, the intersection between thoughts and reality.

It's time to add the third key component of the system we are creating to turn dreams into reality: PLANS.

From a general perspective, planning is the process to identify limitations or constraints, the two most important life constraints being TIME & SPACE.

As the laws of physics dictate, a person can only be in one place at one time.

Let that statement marinate in your mind as we continue to discuss the purpose of planning while we reflect on some examples of typical everyday planning:

"I have a dentist appointment at 1pm, so I need to leave at (time)"

"Yes, I can meet you at (place) at (time)"

"I only have 30 min to eat lunch before my next meeting"

"I will spend all weekend working on this at home"

"Let me check my calendar to see if we can meet this week or next week"

"I wish I could be there but I will be out of town, so let me make sure (person) goes instead".

As you can see, most of our quick planning decisions involve defining the two constraints of TIME & SPACE (place).

As a general rule, always remember that if one of these two is missing, it is not yet a plan. It's what people tend to call "wishful thinking", or as we saw in chapter 1 & 2 is either and idea at the Dream stage or as a Vision statement waiting for additional clarity.

Time Bound Plans vs the Right Timing for our Plans

Since making plans forces us to make a decision on TIME & PLACE for starters, many of our Dreams and Visions keep getting delayed.

Tomorrow turns into next week, which then turns into next month or next year and as we keep delaying the "TIME & PLACE related decisions", Dreams waiting to be realized never get the attention they deserve in the planning process.

The Cyclical Nature of Planning

There is plenty of research and literature around topics like procrastination, fear of commitment and many more reasons for failing to plan, so we will avoid the pitfalls derived from behavioral or psychological obstacles related to planning by approaching planning from the lessons learned in the realm of modern manufacturing and technology.

Back in the 1950s, after World War II, W. Edwards Deming was sent to Japan by the United States government to assist with the reconstruction efforts and to advise Japanese companies on quality management and statistical methods. Deming's teachings had a significant impact on Japanese industry and contributed to Japan's post-war economic recovery. The Toyota manufacturing system became world renowned in the 80s allowing the car industry and many others after that to revamp their approaches to manufacturing.

What made Deming's influence so powerful? His approach was profound but simple. A four step process known as the PDCA cycle that stands for: Plan, Do, Check and Adjust.

The practicality of this method has been fundamental for worldwide organizations to radically change their approach for "problem solving" and "testing new ideas" needed for innovation and continuous improvement, yet it is simple enough for anyone to apply this approach to personal planning habits.

Take for example "cooking at home" by using the system we call 'kitchen' as explained in the introduction of this book. Let's say you want to try a new recipe. You might need to try several times before you reach the point where you are completely satisfied with the taste of your new discovered recipe.

By using the PDCA cycle, you start by planning what you are going to do, then just do it. Tasting and eating your recipe will allow you to check your expectations and based on the outcome, decide if any adjustments are needed to be done next time you try the recipe. The more times you do it, the more satisfying your experience will be making this recipe. One recipe at a time, using a reliable and consistent system, your culinary dreams will come true and delight those around you that get a piece of your dream.

Completing the Full Cycle

Besides considering the constraints of TIME & SPACE while planning, most people struggle with not completing the full PDCA cycle of their plans.

We all have tried doing something that didn't go well and the "bad taste" of a failed experience kept us from even wanting to "Check" or "Adjust". Stopping after the "Do" step, when the experience didn't go as expected can be a result of different things like fear, pain, shame, but the truth is that without the "Check" step of the cycle, the "learning" that should come from any experience hinders and impacts our ability to keep getting better at planning and completing the full cycle.

Acknowledging and Embracing Failure

When FAILURE is seen as part of the possible outcomes in our planning process, we anticipate that something positive will come out of it - the learning from a failed experience is just as precious as a successful execution of a plan. Learning to embrace "failure" allows us to move on faster and protect our mind from the real enemy: Defeat.

Failure vs Defeat: What is the difference

As you have seen so far in this book, using keywords and their meaning in the correct order and sequence makes our system powerful. Not doing so, will be the equivalent of choosing the "wrong storage" for a perishable item in the kitchen. Storing meat or dairy in the pantry instead of the refrigerator is a minor oversight with bigger consequences.

Applying the same logic to our "Dream Making System", is important for learning to differentiate between the following key terms: Failure and Defeat.

You can look up the words and dig deeper into their meanings but here is a practical way of using these two words as part of your new vocabulary for planning success:

Failure is objective while Defeat (giving up) is subjective.

In other words, failure can be viewed objectively as a temporary setback or a learning opportunity, whereas defeat, often associated with giving up or surrendering, is a subjective interpretation of one's circumstances or mindset.

This idea becomes very clear when watching a toddler learning how to walk. The only way we all learned to walk was by experiencing literal failure, over and over. So, if we learned to walk most likely it was because we decided to get up again, never experiencing defeat in our minds as we kept trying and striving for the goal of walking like the adults and other kids around us.

TAKE ACTION: STEP 3

For your Dream(s) & Vision statements on their path to becoming a plan, do the following:

1)Add TIME & SPACE constraints to your vision sentence by narrowing down to possible times and places.

2) Don't worry about HOW you will make things happen. That will come later in the book.

3) If applicable, make at least two versions of your plan: PLAN A & PLAN B. This will allow you to consider more than one alternative and keep your mind open to different options for implementing the same dream.

Here is an example:

Plan A:

I could travel to **Italy and Greece the first two weeks of July** *BECAUSE* _motivation (why)_

Plan B:

I could travel to **Venice the first week of September** *BECAUSE* _motivation (why)_

As we conclude this chapter, remember that Planning and resilience is not just about bouncing back from setbacks, but about rising stronger each time. Embrace the journey ahead, knowing that failure is not the end but a stepping stone toward success. With each setback, we gain valuable lessons that propel us closer to our dreams. Stay determined, for the path to turning dreams into reality awaits your unwavering commitment.

Chapter Four

Goals - Reality Check

"Goals are dreams with deadlines."
- Diana Scharf Hunt

As you get better at practicing the PDCA cycle for planning small things like cooking, or other recurring life activities, you will begin to notice that setting Goals will be a helpful skill to develop as your plans increase in length, complexity and impact.

But not every plan needs to have "written goals" to be executed. Some goals might be subjective ideas in our mind and not writing them are not necessarily blockers for a plan to be successful. For example, when a mother walks into the kitchen, she just "knows" what her goal is when making breakfast for her kids before taking them to school. She does not need to write down the "Goals for her Plan" to make breakfast every morning although in her mind these goals might need daily adjustments, depending on factors like time crunch, mood, available ingredients, etc.

Going forward, we will describe "unwritten goals or plans" as "implicit goals or plans".

Implicit vs Explicit Plans & Goals

According to John Zachman's framework for system architecture created in the 80s, when a document like a business plan is written or verbal contract is written, it has been made "explicit". But transforming an "Implicit" plan and its goals to an "explicit" form takes time and energy. In other words, there is a "cost" attached in taking something implicit into its explicit form.

That is one of the reasons why as humans our minds can operate with implicit plans and goals so we can avoid the cost of time and energy it would require to make them explicit. As long as we don't have to "discuss" or "review" our plans with anyone else, most plans and goals live in our minds in their implicit form.

Now consider when a teenager wants to ask his/her parents permission to go out with friends. His/her "implicit plans and goals" need to be brought to light as part of the communication with the parents.

"Where are you going? Who else is going? Are you going somewhere else after that? What time will you be back?", is the line of interrogation the teenager might be subjected to by caring parents who want to be made aware of the whereabouts (TIME & SPACE) of someone under their responsibility.

Although the responses "might not be written on paper", making the plans and goals "verbally explicit" creates the necessary evidence for two things: Transparency and Accountability.

Transparency and Accountability

Just the way a teenager is forced to make certain decisions when making plans and setting some goals that need to be communicated to the parents, each of us has a set of beliefs, values and principles that allow us to confirm if your plans and goals get "a green light" for execution.

"What time will you be back", asks the mom.

"I don't really know", answers the teenager

"Be back before 9 pm", responds the dad

"Really? What about 10 pm?" replies the teenager

"Ok, but no later than that", concludes the father.

The transparency of an EXPLICIT Plan and its corresponding Goals, whether written or just verbal, allows for identifying "gaps" or "missing" details to make our plans successful.

While a teenager has in mind only a number of things that he/she wants to do when going out, the parents want to make sure that other elements like safety are included. We all know that the interactive nature of a parent-child relationship relies on the intangible element of trust, and while the word "trust" might not be mentioned during the conversation, the line of questioning most likely will be based on the nature and level of trust in the relationship.

Do You Trust Yourself? Should You Trust Yourself?

We won't go into a lot of detail on the topic of trust as it is a deep and complex subject matter but just to make sure it is clear to support our system for making dreams come true, use the following rule of thumb in mind.

The less you trust yourself to make a specific dream come true, the more explicit your plan and goals have to be to make it happen.

Trust is usually linked to experience. Good or bad experiences. If you are planning a big trip this year, your level of trust will be based on your past big trip experiences. If they were good, you will feel confident to make your

Plan and Goals for the next trip even if they are implicit in form. But if the past big trip experiences didn't turn out as good, it is time to complete the PDCA cycle and write down the lessons learned from past experiences.

What went wrong? What needs to be adjusted for the next trip? As you prepare to make your next big trip dream come true, make sure the Plan and its Goals are written this time to spot possible issues or missing elements.

The Interactive Nature of Plans and Goals

Setting explicit goals and plans can be determined based on the "cost" or perceived "potential benefit" of the plan. A big dinner, a career move, a big trip or buying a house; the more you risk to gain or lose, will help determine how much time and energy you should invest in planning and setting goals and making them explicit.

This is where things might get messy and complicated as we deal with the busyness of life. Finding time to even get started with Planning and Goal setting could be the first challenge for many of us, but hopefully if you have read so far in this book, your commitment to make this happen will keep you on the right path.

The second obstacle for many is that even if they are willing to spend the time and energy to plan and set goals, they could be using a broken system or no system at all.

"Making Plans" and "Setting Goals" should be an interactive fun skill that every person should have since we depend on it to navigate the journey of life successfully.

The best formula for success using our newly created system is to recognize that making Plans and setting Goals for those plans is interactive in nature.

An easy and fun way to implement this interactive dynamic between PLANS and GOALS is to think of them as two inner characters in your mind holding an engaging dialog. Think back to when you were a young kid playing with your toys (action figures, dolls, stuffed animals) and all the amazing dreams, plans and goals that your character -the good, the bad and the ugly, will engage in endless adventures unbound by your creativity, curiosity and imagination.

Role playing to make sure the internal dialog happens is more important that you think. Another helpful technique will be to use the analogy of the teenager/parent conversation shown before where the teenager represents your adventurous PLANNING spirit and the parents represent the authoritative nature of GOAL setting, digging deeper to prevent for execution gaps and misalignment with personal values.

TAKE ACTION: STEP 4

1) Take the Plan A or Plan B you worked on at the end of chapter 3 and a blank sheet of paper

2) Divide the sheet of paper in two vertical columns with the left column for your PLANS and the right column for your GOALS.

3) Start a dialog in your head role playing between PLANS & GOALS, with GOALS being the "authority" figure that knows you deeply and keeps a check on your beliefs, values, sanity and responsibilities.

4) Let PLANS come up with options and ideas that GOALS needs to agree to, question or refuse.

5) You don't need to write the whole dialog, but the key words that come from each side.

Plan A:

I could travel to Italy and Greece the first two weeks of July BECAUSE _motivation (why)_

Plan B: I could travel to Venice the first week of September BECAUSE _motivation (why)_

Sample dialog in your head:

PLANS (Teenager)	GOALS (Parent)
I plan to go to Italy this summer	Ok, what cities do you want to visit?
At least two	Which ones?
Not sure yet, Venice and Rome for sure	Any other?
Maybe Florence	How much time are you thinking?
3-5 days per city	Sounds good.

Sample notes on your sheet:

PLANS (Teenager)	GOALS (Parent)
Go to Italy this summer	Country to visit: Italy
Options for cities to visit: Venice, Rome, Florence	Cities: Two or Three
3-5 day per city	Time: 9-15 days

As we wrap up this chapter, it's crucial to grasp the evolving landscape of goal setting and planning. While some plans may thrive with implicit goals, others demand explicit articulation to ensure success in our endeavors.

Understanding the difference between implicit and explicit plans and corresponding goals empowers us to appreciate the value of transparency and accountability in our pursuits.

Additionally, trust in oneself plays a pivotal role in determining the level of detail required in our plans and goals. Remember, the interactive nature of plans and goals invites us to engage in a dynamic dialogue, much like characters in a story, guiding us through life's journey with clarity and purpose.

Embrace this interactive approach, and let the dialogue between your plans and goals propel you toward realizing the dreams of the 'New You'.

Chapter Five

Habits - Lights, Camera, Action!

"Vision without execution is just hallucination."
- Thomas Edison

Imagine your life as a movie, with dreams, visions, plans, and goals serving as the script. It's a captivating tale filled with excitement, challenges, and triumphs, yet until now, it remains confined to the pages of that script. Just as a movie doesn't come to life until the cameras start rolling and the actors take their places, our dreams remain dormant until we take action.

In this chapter, we will explore the crucial role of Habits as the driving force behind turning those scripts into real-life blockbusters and the last key element for our system to turn dreams into reality.

Lights, camera, action! These three words signal the beginning of a journey from imagination to reality. Similarly, our dreams, visions, plans, and goals represent the blueprint for our aspirations. However, without action, they remain mere figments of our imagination, waiting for their moment in the spotlight. Habits, like the actors on a stage, step into the scene to breathe life into those dreams, transforming them from abstract ideas into tangible achievements.

Just as every movie relies on a talented cast and crew to bring the story to life, our journey towards realizing our dreams depends on the habits we cultivate. Habits are both the actor waiting to jump on stage as well as the behind-the-scenes crew that ensure each scene unfolds according to the script. They provide the structure and consistency needed to execute our plans and achieve our goals.

New Habits: The New Actors Ready to Steal the Spotlight

As you might recall from the preface describing the story of my early years in Seattle after my move from Monterrey, Mexico in 2015, starting life in a completely different city, far away from everyone I knew, allowed me to free myself from many constraints and beliefs I had about myself and my way of life up to that point.

The initial assumption of my stay being limited to only one year, added a sense of urgency for taking advantage of the opportunities in front of me. It would have been fairly easy for me to stick to my old habits and stay in my comfort zone, but this opportunity was uniquely a "one in a lifetime" opportunity and I couldn't resist not taking full advantage of it while it lasted.

"Carpe Diem" became my modus operandi. I could not leave something for "tomorrow", so I learned to live in the moment and push my limits beyond my comfort zone, which became easier since my comfort zone pretty much had disappeared when I landed in a completely new city.

Pushing the limit of my dreams and aspirations allowed me to experience things that most likely I wouldn't have learned or done if had stayed where I lived for 30 years, like learning to snowboard, learning to partner dance (salsa, bachata, west coast swing, ki-zomba), learning to windsurf, learning about plants and gardening, while advancing my career to reach three major milestones.

Things are always easier said than done. Making any of these dreams happen involved some major life adjustments and refocus of time and energy. In the next section I will share more about how growing new habits made it all possible, including some practical advise that you might be able to apply on your personal journey.

Key Lessons Learned about Habits

If my experience of nine years can be reduced to few lessons regarding Habits they will be the following:

New habits can only exist when you decide to say goodbye to old habits that no longer serve you.

As mentioned in previous chapters, Time and Space are two constraints that force us to decide what we need to prioritize in our life. Decisions that involve sacrificing old habits is crucial for the success of the New You.

The easiest way to "grow" new habits is to design and build the "Habitat" for them to grow.

Just like parents expecting a baby prep their home to welcome the new member of the family by acquiring specific furniture and deciding on the spaces around the house required for baby-specific-activities, to succeed in growing a new habit you should anticipate and design a "habit-friendly" space at home. Learning a new skill like playing an instrument, cooking, reading, gardening, starting a new business, etc. will be easier if you can designate the "habitat" for it. Compare the easy access most people have at home to watch tv by carefully placing it in a space that will be comfortable and quick to turn on by using a remote. Access to the "tv & movie watching habitat" makes it simple to access and many times hard to escape when that old habit faces competition of newly born habits.

Ask yourself, if kept your TV stored in a box in a closet and every time you wanted to watch it you had to take it out of the box, set it up and use it for a couple of hours and then put it back in the box and inside the closet again, how often will you watch it?

Most likely the hours of watching TV will be reduced drastically, not because watching TV is a hard skill but because the prep required to do it takes so much energy and time.

Now apply this logic to a new habit. Getting to the new habit and not the habit itself will many times be the blocker to your success.

Grow Unexpected Habits that Bring you Joy and Purpose

I remember when back on January 1st of 2021 I met a group of runners in Kirkland, WA. I went to observe and watch people take the "polar plunge" which meant people will get into the cold winter waters of Lake Washington as the first activity of the new year.

I had heard about this being a big thing in the Seattle area but had missed it several times. Finally I was there in Kirkland this time to witness the people that I considered crazy and brave enough to get into freezing cold water.

It turned out to be a small scale event that year as we were all coming out of the year of the pandemic 2020, so there was not a large crowd as I had heard it used to be, only small groups of people and friends getting ready to take the plunge.

I remember seeing a group of runners warming up so I approached one of the guys and asked if they were going to jump into the water. He replied that they will run to warm up for about 30 min. and then go into the water. Without any hesitation he asked me if I would join them. I immediately replied that I didn't come prepare with clothes to get in the water and he said very calmly that if I went home to change and be back in 30 min. I could join them.

I didn't have to think about it twice. I got in my car, drove home, put on my bathing suit and grabbed additional clothes to change afterwards as well as a couple of towels. As I was driving back I just kept thinking that although I was not expecting to get into the water that day, I would regret not doing it more, that actually trying it out.

You see, my hesitation for not doing it that year was that I had never met anyone who had actually done it, so fear of the unknown and how my body might react to getting into freezing water was my main concern. I was not going to do it alone and jeopardize my health but now that a group of "like-minded-crazy" people had invited me to join, there was a sense of security that came from seeing actual relatable human beings that looked just like me and were exciting to take the plunge. If anything went wrong "they" should know what to do, was the calming thought in the back of my mind to my fear of trying something new and un-thinkable for a Mexican guy who grew up in near the tropical waters of Tampico and knew that "no one" is supposed to get into the ocean water during the winter. You just have to wait for the weather to get warmer, was the predetermined assumption I grew up with, which was fighting to stay strong to keep me off the water that day, but now that the "voices" of my new crazy friends were louder, old me and his fears was ready to relax, sit back and see what happened.

The rest of the experience went by quickly. It was one of those things that happened so fast that almost seemed just like a dream. Thankfully, nothing bad happened. The water was cold but didn't seemed as freezing as I had anticipated. Maybe it was the adrenaline rush that came with the fun of running like crazy people into the water with a bunch of strangers that momentarily had become my best friends. 'Old Me' and 'New Me' shook hands. 'New Me' had a story to tell now and 'Old Me' was happy to pass on the baton and allow '2021 New Me' to see what new experiences could be waiting for the 364 remaining days of this new year.

What happened in the following months after the Jan 1st polar plunge was something completely unexpected, but an obvious sequel to the "breakthrough that had taken place in my mind.

I decided to start meeting the same group of runners every Saturday morning to join . I had no expectations of how long will I do it. I just enjoyed the bond that came from the plunge and decided to continue experiencing a bit of that on a weekly basis. It didn't turn out to be easy because running in the

Seattle area still under winter conditions was of course beyond my comfort zone, but compared to plunge seemed hard but not unattainable. The potential benefits of running in the cold weather fueled my curiosity to figure out what drove this small group of runners giving me the motivation to take the next step.

At first I thought it was only joining the Saturday run, but it turn out that after the first time I met them to run, they talked about the January challenge of running 1 mile a day. After briefly considering it, I decided I should give it a try. I was in for a nice surprise.

I really had not run since I was in my 20s, and I would only do it as a way to stay fit in order to play basketball which was the sport I practice and enjoyed since high school. Running for the sake of running had always seemed beyond my comfort zone, so I never considered myself "a runner".

I remember setting up everything at home if I really wanted this 1-mile-a-day thing to happen since it was not a habit for me. Although running a mile took me between 9-10 min. the added effort to prepare for it mentally, change into running gear, making sure not to waste time looking for my running shoes each day became almost as important as the run itself. In my mind, the prep for a new 10 min. activity should take no more than 10% of the time of the activity, which meant having a 1 min. prep. Of course this was a made up rule by 'Old Me' who was fighting hard to make sure I wouldn't try something I was going to fail at.

After the first week I had it all figured out. The exact place for my running shoes and clothes, what to wear on the days it was cold and rainy and the right phone app to track my route and the time for each daily run.

I successfully completed the January challenge and decided I should not stop even if the group didn't have a February challenge. I felt so energized with the first month's breakthrough, so imitating an experienced surfer, I just "rode that wave" as long as I could. It wasn't until mid April that I missed my first day of running a mile. Looking back at a successful three and a half month stretch was mind blowing!!! 'New Me' felt motivated, energized and on fire while 'Old Me' kept making peace with this new reality. The "runner in me" was having the time of his life taking the center stage as the newly introduced character. Introducing this "new character" to family and friends was also a fun experience.

Although moving to Texas later that year impacted the consistency of this newly formed habit, something more important had happened. Like the characters in a TV series that show up for specific episodes and parts of the story, I realized that I can now bring back "1-mile-a-day" guy into any chapter or season without great effort. And the energy that this character brought to my life had allowed me to give life to other habits, that I now refer to as "cast members" ready to take the stage in my life as needed to support what is going on at any given time with the added ability to shuffle overlapping priorities forced by TIME & PLACE constraints.

In other words, I don't need to run a mile everyday, but I can run a mile any day when I need to, and to me that is more powerful than doing something as a routine or feeling bad because I was not able to run a mile any certain day.

Grow habits that support the creation of other habits adding a multiplying effect to your actions.

I hope you can grasp from this previous story that not all habits are created equal. Although new habits can be formed and could be short lived, there are certain habits that are fundamental to allow other habits to grow and emerge.

Like the "behind-the -scenes" crew, certain habits rarely seem take center stage in your life but without them the flashy and cool new actors would not know what to do.

My "run-a-mile" habit guy is totally dependent on my "clean-up-and-organize" habit guy. The encounter with the group of run-

ners on the polar plunge day would have never have happened if my "talk-to-strangers"
habit guy had not showed up that day, and so
on.

As you analyze and reflect on your life and
habits, figure out which habits could be
considered 'back-stage' but fundamental for
your new habits to be brought to life and take
the center stage.

TAKE ACTION: STEP 5

It's time to analyze what are the HABITS needed to make one or more of your Dreams come true.

1)Start making a list of your current HABITS.

2) These are actions or patterns that you do consistently daily, weekly, monthly.

3) Take a piece of paper and divide it with a horizontal line in the middle

4) Classify your HABITS according to how frequently they happen in your life with the ones that happen more frequently (daily) closer to the top and the ones that happen less frequently towards the bottom.

Here are a few examples:

TOP: Waking up early from Mon-Fri

MIDDLE: Water Plants weekly

BOTTOM: Stay up to binge watch a series

Being honest with yourself is a key part of this process. Self analysis and introspection is not always pretty, but willing to start this process is fundamental to your success.

Habits: The characters that will play out your Dreams.

As described at the beginning of this chapter, Dreams, Vision, Plans and Goals can be seen as the script for the movie of your future life, but your habits will make sure your dreams can be executed.

If it makes it easier to identify your habits write them out as a cast member in your life as you saw me doing it in this chapter.

CHARACTERS / CAST MEMBERS:

Clean-up guy

Gardening guy

Book Reading guy

Exercise guy

Shopping guy

Finance and budget guy

Netflix - TV guy

Make Breakfast guy

and so on…

The above list will remind you of the "credits" that you see at the end of a movie.

Although there might be a few main characters, the full cast and crew members needed to make it all happen can be quite extensive…

your life it no different.

Chapter Six

Dreams to Habits Template

N ow that we're well-versed in the components of our dream-realization system, let's shift the focus onto the stage of action. As we delve into the spotlight of aspiration, discover how the components seamlessly come alive, ready for their close-up in the grand production of your dreams. Now that we've unraveled the essence of our unique dream-realization system, let's bring it all together in an easy to use template that you can use over and over.

DREAMS

VISION

PLANS & GOALS

HABITS

I've deliberately laid out these words in a top-to-bottom sequence, each layer revealing a detailed aspect of our journey.

Picture it like this: at the top, we have "Dreams," as abstract as fluffy clouds hovering in the sky. As we descend, the landscape transforms, and "Vision" materializes with the vibrant hues of a beautiful horizon.

Segueing down, "Plans & Goals" nestle in the middle, mirroring the intermediary realm where decisions and aspirations converge. Here, the landscape is a blend of possibilities, akin to the broad expanse of a horizon.

Finally, we reach the tangible ground of "Habits," depicted by the lush, green meadows. These habits, like the verdant grass, root our dreams in reality, forming the bedrock of our journey.

Picture this mental landscape: the heavens above echo with Dreams & Vision, the middle ground resonates with Plans and Goals, while the earthly meadows signify the Habits that anchor our aspirations.

In framing this visual narrative, we carve three horizontal sections:

THINK

DECIDE

ACT

where each layer contributes to the comprehensive canvas of our dream-realization journey.

Within the three layers, our five key words take their place:

THINK layer includes: DREAMS & VISION

DECIDE layer includes: PLANS & GOALS

ACT layer includes: HABITS

This intentional arrangement forms a harmonious and practical template, were each layer contributes uniquely to our dream-realization journey.

As we explore the interplay of thoughts, decisions, and actions, the convergence of these elements creates a dynamic framework for turning aspirations into reality.

"Dreams to Habits" template

THINK	**DREAMS**	
	VISION	
DECIDE	**PLANS**	**GOALS**
ACT	**HABITS**	

In this visual representation, it's essential to highlight the intentional pairing of

Nouns: Dreams, Vision, Plans, Goals & Habits

with

Verbs: Think, Decide, Act.

This deliberate combination of nouns and verbs within our three layers signifies the dynamic nature of the dream-realization journey. The seamless interplay of these elements showcases the power of deliberate reflection, strategic choices, and purposeful steps. Together, these actions drive our dreams closer to reality, demonstrating the tangible impact of our thoughtful efforts.

The Game of Connecting "Dreams to Habits".

Now that you know all the parts of the template, think of like a board game for turning dreams into habits.

You can start by reflecting on your personal HABITS and writing them down in the bottom rectangle—your daily, weekly, and monthly routines.

As suggested at the end of Chapter 5, inject some fun into this process by portraying your habits as characters in the action movie of your everyday life. Instead of merely writing "cooking" try "Chef" or "Cook". Instead of "exercising," consider "Fitness Coach". Coming up with fun characters to describe the daily scenes of your life is a powerful tool.

Don't worry worry about perfection; the characters will evolve naturally as you this more often. Begin with 3-5 "habit characters" and proceed to the next step.

Shift your focus to the top of the board—the Dreams box. Remember, as you continue living, your mind will endlessly swirl with countless DREAMS, an inherent trait of our imaginative selves. Taking a moment to pause is crucial if you want to succeed!

Identify the recurring dreams that persistently capture your attention. Choose one or two and write them at the top of the board.

Apply the format from the end of chapter 1 as the launching pad for further exploration:

"If money and time were not a problem, I would (want)_____"

OR

"If money and time were not a problem, I should (need)_____"

Now, the thrilling challenge continues as you fill the remaining boxes. Your objective is to guarantee that the HABITS anchored at the bottom align seamlessly with the actions required to execute your PLANS and GOALS.

Until you conduct this top-to-bottom analysis and discovery, the success of your dreams from a planning or decision perspective might have some gaps, but you won't know until all the boxes are filled.

This straightforward yet potent game offers a tangible framework to synchronize your daily habits with the aspirations inscribed at the top, steering you towards the deliberate execution of your dreams.

TAKE ACTION: STEP 6

Starting Small while keep Dreaming Big

If you are planning a big trip in a year or two, start by planning small weekend trips. Use the format shown above and fill as many of the boxes as possible for each trip. With every trip you plan, you will be able to identify things that you can improve, problems that you faced, and evaluate how you solved them or how they impacted your trip.

Remember that the most important thing in the long term will be the "New Habits" that you identify as needed to support each of your Dreams. You will find out how amazing the power of small things in the form of Habits can impact either in a positive or negative way your big plans and goals.

Chapter Seven

Mastering the System

E quipped with a "modern kitchen-like system" for transforming dreams into reality, you now stand at the threshold of an exciting journey.

Much like learning to cook, utilizing this system requires time, practice, and the gradual development of skills to evolve into a "master chef." Begin with modest steps, gather experiences, and iterate the process.

Real-life applications for the dream-realization system, opens the door to a diverse realm of personal projects, each representing a unique facet of your aspirations.

As we begin applying this system to identify new dreams and take the practical steps recommended in each chapter we will be faced with some big questions about the large spectrum of dreams, ranging from the significant milestones like buying a house and pursuing higher education to the transformative experiences of changing careers, getting in shape, studying for a master's degree, and delving into newfound hobbies.

Personal Projects: A Spectrum of Dreams

By exploring a few types of common personal projects that seem to align with things "most people do" given our current modern standards and opportunities, we hope to uncover the universal principles described in this book as well as the habits that need to be aligned for successful dream realization.

Even if any of the following "personal projects" do not apply to your particular situation, the intention is to inspire you, offering additional insights into the dynamic interaction between dreams and the deliberate actions and habits that bring them to fruition.

Remember that these are sample categories that you can use to practice with the "Dreams to Habits" template to begin adjusting and enhancing the methods you have been using so far for planning and executing your dreams.

A. Buying a House

Planning and Financial Considerations: Embarking on the journey of buying a house involves meticulous planning and financial foresight. Begin by assessing your financial landscape, determining a budget, and outlining your home ownership goals. Consider factors such as mortgage rates, loan options, and potential future expenses.

Decision-Making Processes: Navigating the intricate landscape of home buying requires thoughtful decision-making processes. From selecting the right neighborhood to choosing a property that aligns with your lifestyle, each decision plays a pivotal role in shaping your home ownership journey. Explore strategies for evaluating property options, conducting thorough inspections, and making informed choices.

Executing the Steps Toward Home ownership: With a solid plan and informed decisions in place, it's time to execute the steps toward home ownership. Dive into the practical aspects of the process, from submitting mortgage applications and negotiating deals to handling legalities and completing the transaction.

Self-reflection: What habits seem to be missing from your current way of life to make this type of dream, buying a house or investing in real estate, a reality?

B. Changing Careers or Getting a New Job

Assessing Skills and Interests: Initiating a career change or seeking a new job involves a thorough self-assessment of your skills, interests, and aspirations. Reflect on your strengths, identify areas of passion, and evaluate the alignment of your current skills with your desired career path.

Exploring New Opportunities: The journey to a new career begins with exploration. Delve into various industries, research emerging trends, and identify opportunities that resonate with your aspirations. Understand the job market, networking strategies, and the skills in demand within your chosen field.

Strategically Transitioning to a New Career: Transitioning to a new career requires a strategic approach. Develop a clear transition plan, incorporating steps such as upskilling, networking, and crafting a compelling resume. Learn effective strategies for highlighting transferable skills and positioning yourself as a valuable asset in your chosen field.

Self-reflection: What habits seem to be missing from your current way of life to make this type of dream, career move, a reality?

C. Getting in Shape

Setting Fitness Goals: Embarking on a journey to get in shape begins with setting clear and realistic fitness goals. Identify your desired outcomes, whether it's weight loss, muscle gain, improved endurance, or overall well-being. Establish a timeline and measurable benchmarks to track your progress.

Creating a Personalized Workout Routine: Crafting a personalized workout routine is a key component of the journey to fitness. Tailor your exercise plan to align with your goals, preferences, and fitness level. Explore a variety of workouts, incorporating elements of cardiovascular exercise, strength training, and flexibility.

Integrating Healthy Habits into Daily Life: Achieving and maintaining fitness goes beyond workouts; it involves cultivating healthy habits in your daily life. Explore nutrition strategies, hydration practices, and adequate rest to complement your exercise routine. Learn to navigate challenges such as time constraints and stress, integrating sustainable habits into your lifestyle.

Self-reflection: What habits seem to be missing from your current way of life to make this type of dream, physical fitness, a reality?

D. Studying for a Master's Degree

Identifying Academic Interests: Pursuing a master's degree requires a deep exploration of your academic interests and passions. Reflect on your career goals, areas of expertise, and the subjects that ignite your intellectual curiosity.

Researching and Applying to Programs: Navigating the process of studying for a master's degree involves thorough research and strategic applications. Explore various programs, consider factors such as accreditation, faculty, and program structure. Understand the application process, requirements, and deadlines.

Managing the Academic Journey and Workload: Successfully studying for a master's degree requires effective management of the academic journey and workload. Develop strategies for time management, organization, and maintaining a healthy work-life balance. Understand the expectations of graduate-level studies and learn techniques for staying focused and motivated throughout your academic pursuits.

Self-reflection: What habits seem to be missing from your current way of life to make this type of dream, academic growth, a reality?

E. Starting a Hobby

Discovering Personal Interests: Initiating a new hobby begins with discovering your personal interests and passions. Reflect on activities that bring joy, excitement, or curiosity. Explore uncharted territories and consider hobbies that align with your values and preferences.

Gathering Necessary Resources: Once you've chosen a hobby, the next step involves gathering the necessary resources and tools. Whether it's art supplies, sports equipment, or musical instruments, understanding what you need to get started is essential.

Progressing from Novice to Enthusiast: Transitioning from a novice to an enthusiast in your hobby requires patience, practice, and a gradual learning curve. Set achievable milestones, seek guidance from experts or online communities, and celebrate your progress along the way.

Self-reflection: What habits seem to be missing from your current way of life to make this type of dream, starting a new hobby, a reality?

Chapter Eight

Conclusion

Embracing the Script of Your Life

Now that you have been able get familiar with my story, hopefully you will better understand my perspective and the reasons that motivated me to come up with the system and essential elements I have shared with you in this book.

Considering each of our lives as a grand production, we are both the playwrights and the protagonists, shaping our narratives with dreams, visions, plans, and goals, awaiting for the true magic to happens when we step onto the stage and turn those scripts into reality.

Lights, camera, action! Keep these words in mind as you continue your personal life transformation—from imagination to tangible achievement, never under estimating the pivotal role of habits as the unsung heroes, both actors and behind-the-scenes crew, breathing life into our aspirations. Like a well-rehearsed cast, our habits provide structure and consistency, ensuring each scene unfolds according to the script of our dreams.

It is time now for you to uncovered key lessons about your current dreams and the personal habits that resonate with your new reality.

Make deliberate choices to bid farewell to old habits that no longer serve you as a crucial step in crafting the "New You." Create habit-friendly spaces, the habitat which becomes the stage where new habits can flourish, much like a movie set designed for success.

Just like it happen to me, your insight into the unexpected joys and purposes that can arise from cultivating new habits can be truly inspirational.

Seek for "polar plunge" opportunities that might be scary or beyond your comfort zone, seemingly spontaneous acts ready to unveil a series of events with the power to transform into a sequel of breakthroughs.

These opportunities will allow you to challenge yourself with things that might seem small and achievable like my "1-mile-a-day" character, which I use to showcased not only the power of consistency but also the interconnectedness of habits. Some habits, like those behind the scenes, may not take the spotlight but are indispensable for the success of the starring actors.

As the curtain falls on this chapter of your life, remember that not all habits are created equal. Some, the unsung heroes, provide the foundation for others to shine. Even those old but faithful habits like my "clean-up-and-organize" habit guy who was essential for the "run-a-mile" habit guy to even exist.

In concluding this script, may you continue to craft a compelling narrative, embracing each scene with the wisdom gained from habits old and new, while discovering the unexpected joys of embracing the unknown, and the enduring impact of habits on the grand stage of life.

The credits roll, but your journey continues. The script is yours to write, the stage yours to command. The story of your life, an ever-evolving masterpiece, awaits the next exciting chapter.

Thank you,

Abner Amador

***

To download a PDF file with the
"Dreams to Habits" template
please visit my website:
abneramador.com

***

If the message and ideas on this book
resonated with you and you have found it
helpful,
I will be grateful for your honest review
on the book's amazon page.

***

Made in United States
Troutdale, OR
02/15/2024